The Journey

of

Monomoy Girl

By W.G. Davis

Copyright © 2021 by W.G. Davis

All rights reserved.

I dedicate this book to all of the micro-share owners of Monomoy Girl.

If you were one of the lucky ones to be able to own a percentage of this amazing racehorse, you can fill in your owner information below.

NAME

PURCHASE DATE

NUMBER OF SHARES PURCHASED

MyRacehorse ORDER #

The story of Monomoy Girl could not be told without starting from her championship roots.

Many people don't know that Monomoy Girl's roots go back to Secretariat and Seattle Slew.

Sire: Bold Reasoning Dam: My Charmer

Foal: Seattle Slew

Sire: Secretariat Dam: Lassie Dear

Foal: Weekend Surprise

Sire: Seattle Slew Dam: Weekend Surprise

Foal: A.P. Indy

Sire: A.P. Indy Dam: Preach

Foal: Pulpit

Sire: Pulpit Dam: Tap Your Heels

Foal: Tapit

Sire: Tapit Dam: Winning Call

Foal: Tapizar

Sire: Tapizar Dam: Drumette

Foal: Monomoy Girl

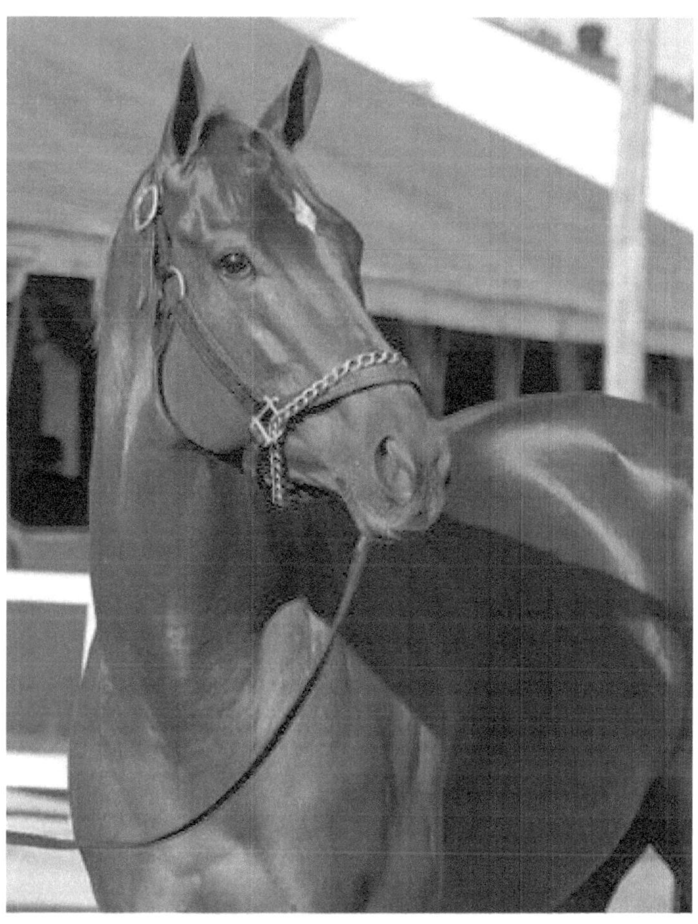

Monomoy Girl

Now let's first take a look at Monomoy Girl's championship roots.

Part One
Secretariat

Secretariat with Jockey, Ron Turcotte, Groom, Eddie Sweat and owner, Penny Chenery - 1973

Many people know Secretariat from the 2010 Walt Disney movie, "Secretariat"

But Secretariat's life is more than just a Disney movie of a racehorse.

Secretariat was foaled in Doswell Virginia in the early morning of March 30th, 1970 at Meadow Farm. Secretariat was sired by Bold Ruler from Somethingroyal.

In an attempt to save her ill father's farm, Penny Chenery left her life in Denver, Colorado.

Despite her family's suggestion of selling off the farm and just walking away, she stayed to attempt and save what she could of the farm.

Penny acquired Secretariat in a coin toss when they were dividing up the potential offspring with mares bred to his sire, Bold Ruler.

Penny at first was unsure if the foal, Secretariat, would ever be a winner.

Secretariat as a foal

Even at a very young age, Secretariat was a massive colt, who was quick to stand and nurse.

Over the years, it has been said that Penny kept notes on their horses and foals.

And the one-word note next to Secretariat's name was, "Wow!'

Secretariat's trainer, Lucien Laurin, was ready to retire when he joined Penny, soon clinching five of six consecutive Triple Crown wins between Secretariat and his stablemate, Riva Ridge.

Ron Turcotte, Secretariat's jockey for his Triple Crown wins, grew up in Canada working with his father as a lumberjack.

The story of Secretariat and his team fascinated the country over the horse's career as a two and three-year-old.

Together, Ron Turcotte and Secretariat won all three races of the Triple Crown in 1973.

The last time this feat was accomplished was 25 years earlier by Citation who earned the title in 1948.

Ron Turcotte and Secretariat were breaking track records in each race that still stands today.

On May 5, 1973, they won the 99th running of the Kentucky Derby. Secretariat was the first horse to ever win the Derby in under 2 minutes with a time of 1:59.40.

Monarchos in 2001, was the only horse to even come close to Secretariat's record, finishing at an official time of 1:59.97

Secretariat went on to win the 98th running of the Preakness Stakes on May 19, 1973, in 1:53.

For the 105th running of the Belmont Stakes on June 9th, 1973, Secretariat won in just 2:24 by an astounding 31 lengths.

Cameras with the widest lenses were unable to capture Secretariat and the closest horse behind him in the same shot as he crossed the wire.

A New York racing official has been quoted as saying, "He was not a horse, he was Secretariat."

Over his racing career, Secretariat was described as absolute perfection in every way, the way God intended to make a horse.

Secretariat stood at 16.2 with anatomically perfect conformation, and powerful hindquarters, ideal stride biomechanics, with a 24-foot 11-inch stride

In total, Secretariat's racing record consisted of 21 starts with 16 wins, earning $1,316,808 on the racetrack.

Secretariat retired to Claiborne Farm in Paris, Kentucky in 1973 where he stood at stud.

During his time as a stud Secretariat sired 653 offspring including 57 stakes winners, eventually being known as a top broodmare sire of his time.

And one of those foals, when Secretariat was mated with Lassie Dear, was Weekend Surprise.

Lassie Dear would be the first Dam in the Secretariat bloodline to Monomoy Girl.

During his retirement years, Secretariat developed laminitis, a painful and debilitating hoof condition, which was first diagnosed on Labor Day of 1989.

Secretariat's veterinarian Dr. Swerczek said that Secretariat's laminitis was the worst case he had ever seen.

Sadly there was no chance of a cure or improvement and the staff at Claiborne farm realized on the morning of October 4th, 1989 that Secretariat needed to be euthanized.

Because Secretariat was insured, a necropsy (autopsy) was required, despite the obvious answer of his untimely death being laminitis.

However, he needed to examine Secretariat's liver, Kidneys, and feet to confirm and satisfy the insurance company's requirements.

Secretariat's owners wanted Secretariat to have the necropsy close by Claiborne farm and returned for a prepared burial at the farm.

They had dug the grave near his sire, Bold Ruler, and planned on burying him in a silk-lined wooden casket.

It is a common tradition that great racehorses have only their head (intelligence), heart (courage and spirit), and hooves (speed) buried upon their death as a way of memorializing their greatness as a racehorse.

They insisted that Dr. Swerczek perform the necropsy. They had a problem getting a hold of Dr. Swerczek.

Dr. Swerczek's son, Michael, was critically injured at the time and was not expected to live.

Dr. Swerczek had been traveling back and forth to the labs to do what necropsies he could on other horses, and that is the reason why he was not aware of what bad shape Secretariat was in.

When they finally were able to reach him that day, he dropped everything to rush and do the necropsy on Secretariat.

He left his son, not even knowing if he would survive, to do the necropsy. That is how much Secretariat meant to him, and why he did not have his photographing equipment or his scale when he finally arrived.

He simply was not prepared with having all of the necessary equipment that day. There was just no time.

When they brought Secretariat into the lab for the necropsy, there were 8-10 people from the farm that came with him.

Each one of them had plastic bags with them.

They wanted to take every bit of Secretariat back with them to be buried.

During the necropsy, Dr. Swerczek removed Secretariat's heart and set it on the table.

Dr. Kaufman, the resident veterinarian at Claiborne Farm asked,

"Isn't that awfully large?" Dr. Swerczek took a moment, and replied, "It isn't awfully large, and it's the largest heart I have ever seen."

After examining the heart closer they discovered that there were no pathological abnormalities of the heart, typically found in a horse with such an enlarged heart.

It was a perfect heart, everything was just bigger.

The average Thoroughbred's heart is 8-9 lbs.

Secretariat's heart was estimated to be 21-22 lbs., nearly 2.5 times larger than the average heart.

The discovery of Secretariat's oversized heart explained the mystery surrounding how he could be so magnificent.

It was the perfect combination of, his large muscled body, deep chest cavity, and broad girth, paired with his large heart that acted just like an engine in a racecar.

Secretariat's large heart allowed him to receive more oxygen, allowing his muscles to receive optimum oxygen replacement for faster recovery, therefore increasing his stamina.

There has been controversy over the years regarding the discovery of Secretariat's oversized heart and Dr. Swerczek not providing proof, such as photographic evidence of the heart, and not having a scale for the exact weight.

Many have questioned why he didn't preserve the heart.

Secretariat was the exact combination of all that made the perfect racehorse.

Part Two
Seattle Slew

Another standout in the horseracing world of the 70s was Seattle Slew.

He was bought in 1975 as a yearling by Mickey and Karen Taylor of White Swan, Washington, for a relatively modest sum.

And just two short years later in 1977, Seattle Slew became just the 10th horse in history to win the Kentucky Derby, Preakness Stakes, and Belmont Stakes; these are best known as the Triple Crown.

And he was the first to do so with an undefeated record.

Seattle Slew was an undervalued colt who grew up to be one of horseracing's most successful horses in the history of Thoroughbred racing and breeding.

Seattle Slew was gangly but big and with a strong frame. Karen Taylor liked him as soon as she saw him at the Fasig-Tipton July Yearling Sale in Lexington, Kentucky.

He seemed full of energy and power. She and her husband Mickey Taylor were there to buy racehorses in the $10,000-$15,000 range.

When the bidding on the big bay colt went past their $15,000 range, Mickey hesitated, but Karen told him to keep bidding. Ninety seconds after bidding started, they had an animal that would change their lives. They got the horse for $17,500, the most they spent at that day's sale but, as it turned out, an almost unimaginable bargain.

He was born on February 15, 1974, near Lexington, at White Horse Acres, the third foal by his sire, Bold Reasoning, and the first for his dam, My Charmer.

The colt ended up at the Fasig-Tipton auction after being rejected for the more prestigious Keeneland summer yearling sale, partly because his parents had not yet proved their worth in the breeding shed. He also had slight angling out of his front right foot.

Many people saw the flaws in Seattle Slew in a horse that turned out to be perfection.

Before purchasing Seattle Slew, the Taylors had been involved in racing for three seasons, but they were hardly typical racehorse owners.

They were young and from the Pacific Northwest, far from Kentucky's Bluegrass Country, the traditional center of Thoroughbred racing and breeding.

They lived on the Yakama Indian Reservation, in a mobile home, in a town of 600.

Karen and Mickey Taylor became horseracing fans, betting at Yakima Meadows and Longacres. For a third-anniversary present, Mickey promised his wife a racehorse.

They bought their first horse that summer at a Washington Thoroughbred Breeders and Owners Association sale for $5,000. He ran under the name Pearson's Barn, Inc., and made their racing debut and got their first win that December with black and yellow silks that included a drawing of a logging truck.

By the 1975 summer yearling sales in Kentucky, the Taylors owned four winners of stakes races (those in which the owners of the horses contribute to the purse, or prize money, thus attracting better horses than lower-paying races).

They also had met a New York veterinarian named Jim Hill, who tended to racehorses.

Together they formed a corporation called White Horse Investments to acquire more horses.

On Hill's recommendation, the Taylors assigned the horse to Billy Turner, a trainer the vet knew in New York. He was a former steeplechase jockey who had been training horses for about 10 years.

But first, the colt was sent to a farm in Maryland, where they had to get him used to being saddled and ridden, and teaching him to respond to voice and hand commands.

He was nicknamed Baby Huey, after a big and clumsy cartoon character.

He was then moved to Billy Turner's stables at Belmont Park in New York, where the colt acquired an official name. The owners wanted to pay homage to the Taylors' home state and to the swampy area around Fort Meyers, Florida, where Jim Hill was raised.

They settled on the name Seattle Slew, although his handlers more often called him Huey.

Once Turner knew the horse could run, he decided to delay his racing debut and let him add muscle. He also tried to get him to relax, jogging him until he did, before letting him gallop.

Seattle Slew continued to impress his trainer in workouts. It was becoming apparent that Seattle Slew was a special horse.

On September 20, 1976, after most of his fellow 2-year-olds already had raced several times, Seattle Slew made his competitive debut.

Jean Cruguet, a native Frenchman and veteran rider would be his jockey.

Cruguet rode Seattle Slew through the Triple Crown campaign.

The race was at Belmont Park and six furlongs (3/4 of a mile).

Slew initially was established as a 10-1 long shot, meaning a $1 bet on him would pay $10 if he won.

But the word of his speedy workouts had spread. When betting closed, the big dark horse was the 7-5 favorite.

And he didn't disappoint his betters, he won by five lengths.

Seattle Slew's first real test came in the Champagne Stakes on October 16.

It was a showdown with For the Moment, a million-dollar horse.

And not only did Seattle Slew win by 9-3/4 lengths he posted the fastest mile time ever by a 2-year-old at Belmont.

Despite having raced only three times within just 21 days, Seattle Slew won the Eclipse Award as the 1976 champion 2-year-old male and was considered as the early favorite to win the 1977 Kentucky Derby.

In Seattle Slew's debut as a 3-year-old, on March 9, 1977, at Hialeah, he won a seven-furlong allowance race by nine lengths in record time.

Next was the Flamingo Stakes, at 1-1/8 miles Seattle Slew's longest race to date. He won by four lengths.

Then again on April 23 at the Aqueduct racetrack in New York City, in the Wood Memorial Seattle, Slew led all the way and coasted to victory by 3-1/4 lengths.

He had raced six times, all victories and all without being extended. His trainer knew that he was now ready for the biggest show and most prestigious event in horseracing.

The Kentucky Derby, held the first Saturday in May at Louisville's historic Churchill Downs, is the youngest of the three Triple Crown races, but unlike the other two has been run every year since 1875.

The 103rd edition of the "Run for the Roses," as The Kentucky Derby is called, was on May 7, 1977.

Seattle Slew became spooked by the enormous crowd and commotion around him. He began to sweat during the walk from the barn area to the paddock, and when the band played the traditional pre-race anthem, "My Old Kentucky Home," Seattle Slew became jumpy.

In everyone's disbelief, Seattle Slew hesitated when the starting gate opened and then swerved suddenly to the outside, throwing Cruguet off-balance.

When Cruguet was able to regain his footing he was boxed in by other horses.

He responded by barreling through the crowd of horses and soon was running with the leader, For the Moment.

As they entered the home stretch, For the Moment faded. Run Dusty Run mounted a late charge but he just couldn't catch up to Seattle Slew, who won the 103rd edition of The Kentucky Derby by nearly two lengths.

Two weeks later, on May 21, 1977, the 102nd Preakness at Pimlico Race Course in Baltimore, Seattle Slew broke cleanly from the starting gate and quickly was running with the leading horse, Cormorant.

Seattle Slew won by 1-1/2 lengths, relaxing near the finish. Slew's winning time of 1:54-2/5 seconds matched the winning record by Secretariat, the 1973 Triple Crown winner, and was just 2/5 of a second slower than the Preakness record.

The Belmont Stakes presented a different challenge for Seattle Slew, because of its 1-1/2 mile length.

A horse that was fast enough to win the Derby and Preakness might not have the endurance needed to win at the longer distance of The Belmont Stakes.

When Secretariat did it, taking the Belmont by an astounding 31 lengths, he became the first Triple Crown winner in 25 years and only the ninth ever.

Twenty-three times (as of 2018) has a horse has won the first two races but failed to win the Belmont.

A crowd of over 71,000, second-biggest in the event's 109-year history, gathered at Belmont on race day, June 11, 1977.

The track was sloppy after a hard rain but Seattle Slew led all the way, enough so that as he neared the finish line Cruguet broke precedent.

Knowing he would win, the jockey stood up in the stirrups with about 20 yards to go and raised his right arm in victory, a move that would later become customary in comfortable big-race victories.

Seattle Slew finished four lengths ahead of runner-up Run Dusty Run to win the Triple Crown with a perfect record of nine wins in nine starts.

Affirmed won the Crown the following year followed in 2015, by American Pharoah.

And then, just three years later, in 2018, Justify became the 13th Triple Crown winner and, with a career record of six wins and no losses, the first to match Seattle Slew's feat of winning the Crown with an undefeated record.

Seattle Slew developed respiratory problems in the fall of 1977 and didn't race again as a 3-year-old.

He still won Eclipse Awards as Horse of the Year and champion 3-year-old colt.

A serious viral infection kept Seattle Slew from racing during the 1978 winter season.

The owners could have put Slew out to stud then, but they didn't want to deprive the public of the sport's biggest star.

As a four-year-old, Seattle Slew raced only seven times.

On September 16, 1978, the field for the $300,000 Marlboro Stakes at Belmont Park included the 1978 Triple Crown winner, Affirmed.

This race was the first time Triple Crown winners ever competed head to head.

This race was Seattle Slew's first race with a new jockey.

The owners had fired Cruguet after Slew lost by a neck one week earlier in the Paterson Handicap at The Meadowlands Racetrack in New Jersey.

His replacement was the winning rider in the Paterson Handicap race, Angel Cordero Jr.

Although Affirmed was the newer star and a slight betting favorite in the Marlboro Stakes, Seattle Slew took an early lead and held it all the way, ultimately winning by two lengths.

The Triple Crown winners were once again matched two weeks later in the 1-1/2-mile Jockey Club Gold Cup race.

Seattle Slew broke early from the starting gate and had to be reloaded. When the race started, Seattle Slew and Affirmed immediately shared the lead.

Seattle Slew stayed at the front of the pack as they clocked blistering times for the first half-mile.

Suddenly, with a quarter-mile to go, Exceller had a slight lead and all the momentum.

Seattle Slew found new reserves and they pounded toward the finish line together, Seattle Slew was surging as the two horses neared the finish.

The thrilling stretch run ended in a photo finish. The camera showed Exceller had won by a nose.

Although Seattle Slew lost the race, he added to his glowing reputation by showing his strength and determination at the finish, he displayed an extraordinary combination of speed, stamina, and fight.

Even though Seattle Slew lost the race, many consider it the best race of his career.

Seattle Slew raced one more time, winning the Stuyvesant Handicap at Aqueduct on November 11, 1978, and then was sent to stud at Spendthrift Farm near Lexington Kentucky.

At the end of his 1978 race season, Seattle slew retired with a 14-3 record and earnings of nearly $1.21 million and later was given a fourth Eclipse Award, this time as older male champion.

Affirmed narrowly beat him out for Horse of the Year, an honor never denied to a reigning Triple Crown winner.

He was scheduled to be bred to 45 mares in his first season at stud, and the results of that crop and ones to follow only drove his value higher.

Seattle Slew was moved to Three Chimneys Farm near Midway, Kentucky in September 1985, when Spendthrift Farm started having financial problems.

Seattle Slew's offspring continued to command high prices and do well on the track.

In 1989, Slew sired A. P. Indy from a daughter of the 1973 Triple Crown winner Secretariat; their foal went on to be Horse of the Year in 1992.

A. P. Indy is the foal that brings the bloodline of Seattle Slew and Secretariat down to Monomoy Girl.

For more than 20 years after Seattle Slew retired from racing, he was one of the world's most-sought stallions for breeding purposes.

In early 2000, the now 26-year-old Seattle Slew began losing coordination in his hindquarters while walking.

He was given injections to relieve pressure in his arthritic neck joints, but the relief was only temporary.

In April 2000, he underwent surgery to fuse the joints and reduce pressure on his spinal cord. A Bagby Basket was inserted in his neck to help with pressure on his spinal cord.

The surgery was successful, and Seattle Slew returned to stud service the following year.

His stud fee was $150,000 with no guarantee of a foal, but he successfully bred with 43 of 46 mares that year.

His neurological problems returned early in 2002, however.

Slew was removed from stud service in February 2002, and in March a second Bagby Basket was surgically inserted above the first one in Seattle Slew's neck.

By the end of March, Slew was up and walking again. And his sexual interest in the mares had returned, which was a problem for his recovery.

He would get agitated whenever he heard the mares arriving to be bred with other stallions.

It was decided that Seattle Slew needed to be in a quieter setting away from the mares.

In April Seattle Slew was moved to Hill 'n' Dale Farm just outside of Lexington.

Over the next month, Seattle Slew's condition worsened.

The 28-year-old Seattle Slew died at 9 a.m. on May 7, 2002, in Kentucky.

His death was 25 years to the day after he won the Kentucky Derby.

And both times, the Taylors were by his side.

Seattle Slew was buried whole at Hill 'n' Dale with his favorite blanket and a bag of peppermints.

Being buried whole is the highest honor for a winning racehorse.

In 1981, Seattle Slew was inducted into the National Museum of Racing and Hall of Fame.

His offspring and his offspring's offspring keep adding to his legacy as "the people's horse" who became one of the all-time greats.

Seattle Slew sired 1,103 named foals, of which 537 (48.7%) were winners and 111 (10.1%) were stakes winners.

And their foals are legendary horses themselves.

Part Three
A.P. Indy

The primary conduit for the continuation of Seattle Slew's male bloodline has been through A.P. Indy.

A.P. Indy was the leading sire in North America of 2003 and 2006.

A.P. Indy was a son of Seattle Slew. His Dam, Weekend Surprise, by Secretariat, was a multiple graded stakes winner whose first foal, Summer Squall, won the 1990 Preakness Stakes.

Selling for $2.9 million, A.P. Indy was the highest-priced yearling in 1990 at auction.

His new owner, Tomonori Tsurumaki, named the colt in honor of his recently opened Nippon Autopolis, where he hoped to host a Formula One (Indy Car) event.

A.P. Indy won the Belmont Stakes and Breeders Cup Classic before being named US Horse of the Year in 1992.

He went on to lead the North American sire list twice, producing multiple classic winners.

For much of his career, he stood at a stud fee of $300,000.

In February 1994 A.P. Indy would sire Pulpit with Dame Preach.

Pulpit was Monomoy Girl's Great-Grandsire (great-grandfather).

In 2000, A.P. Indy was inducted into the Hall of Fame.

A.P. Indy sired the 2003 Horse of the Year, Mineshaft, Preakness Stakes winner Bernardini and Belmont Stakes winner Rags to Riches.

A.P. Indy's descendants include Tapit, the leading North American sire in 2014, 2015, and 2016.

And also includes multiple American Classic winners such as Tonalist and California Chrome.

In 2014, Seattle Slew's great-great-grandson, and Tapit's son, California Chrome, won the Kentucky Derby and the Preakness.

In 2014, California Chrome was the second Kentucky Derby winner in a row who was a sire-line descendant of Seattle Slew.

On February 21, 2020, A.P. Indy died at the age of 31 at Lane's End Farm in Versailles, Kentucky.

The bloodline from A.P. Indy to Monomoy Girl is as follows:

PULPIT

Sire: A.P. Indy

Dam: Preach

Pulpit's female family traces back to one of Claiborne's foundation mares, Knight's Daughter, the dam of Round Table.

Pulpit won the Fountain of Youth and Blue Grass Stakes before finishing fourth in the 1997 Kentucky Derby.

Pulpit was injured after the 1997 Kentucky Derby and was retired to stud at Claiborne Farm near Paris, Kentucky.

Pulpit lived out his final years at Claiborne Farm until his death on December 6, 2012.

TAPIT

Sire: Pulpit

Dam: Tap Your Heels

An interesting fact about Dam Tap Your Heels; she is inbred to In Reality, a descendant of Man o' War.

She is also a stakes-winning mare by Unbridled.

Tap Your Heels' dam, Ruby Slippers also produced champion sprinter Rubiano and is the third dam of champion Summer Bird.

Tapit was the leading North American sire in 2014, 2015, and 2016.

Tapit is the Grandsire (grandfather) of Monomoy Girl.

Tapit's son, Tonalist, another great-grandson of Seattle Slew, the favored California Chrome another great-grandson of Seattle Slew, in the Belmont Stakes, and stopped his bid for the Triple Crown.

Tonalist went on to win the Peter Pan Stakes in May 2014.

He is the first horse since A.P. Indy in 1992 to win the Peter Pan/Belmont double.

Tapit also sired the winners of the 2016 and the 2017 Belmont Stakes, Creator and Tapwrit respectively.

Tapwrit's Belmont Stakes win marked the third time a son of Tapit had won the Belmont Stakes in four years.

With Tapit's record of siring winning horses, his stud fee steadily increased from the original $15,000.

In 2014, a single share in Tapit, providing a guaranteed breeding right for the rest of his career, was sold for $2.8 million.

This share price made Tapit's total value an estimated $140 million.

For the 2015 breeding season, Tapit's stud fee was $300,000, the same as his Grandsire A.P. Indy's stud fee.

In 2017, Tapit's stud fee was the highest in the United States.

Part Four
Tapizar and Drumette

As we have seen Monomoy Girl comes from a very long pedigree of great racehorses.

Let's take a closer look at her parents Tapizar and Drumette.

TAPIZAR

Sire: Tapit

Dam: Winning Call

As a descendent of some of the world's greatest racehorses, Tapizar wasn't a top-notch racehorse.

As a two-year-old Tapizar ran only four times.

His first race was a maiden Special Weight at Monmouth Park where he ended the race finishing third.

In his second race, he stumbled badly, unseated his rider, and did not finish the race.

His third race was at Churchill Downs. At the start, he broke decently and stayed in the third position almost to the end.

He eventually faded to fourth place at the end of the race.

His fourth and final race was again at Churchill Downs.

He started the race a length behind the leader Ratatat and stayed there for most of the race, but eventually, Tapizar passed Ratatat to take a five-length lead of everyone else at the far turn.

Tapizar finished by more the double at 10 1/2 lengths.

With his impressive win at Churchill Downs the previous race season, many people felt that he would be a good three-year-old runner.

In his three-year-old season, he raced four times.

His first race as a three-year-old was his graded stakes debut, the Sham Stakes at Santa Anita where he won by four and a quarter lengths.

It looked as though Tapizar was starting to live up to his pedigree.

Tapizar tried to make his second graded stakes win in his second race in the Robert B. Lewis Stakes. He took the lead early; unfortunately, he began to tire at the far turn and finished in fifth place.

He suffered a chipped knee after the race and did not race for another eight months.

By October Tapizar had recovered completely and planned to return in an allowance.

Allowance races are exactly what their name implies. Allowances are made or "conditions are set" for the horse to be eligible to run in that race.

After a strong start, he took the lead by the first quarter, keeping the lead by just a length. Then at the far turn, he opened up to win the race by two and a quarter lengths.

With that win, he was able to make his Grade 1 debut in the Breeders' Cup Dirt Mile.

In the Breeders' Cup Dirt Mile, he started fifth and began to move up. He soon moved up to third, but by the end of the race, he faded back to finish in fifth place.

Tapizar finished his three-year-old race season with two wins and two losses.

Tapizar's four-year-old season started just like the third by running in The San Fernando Stakes.

The San Fernando Stakes is a graded stakes race at Santa Anita in January where he won by three and a half lengths.

His second race was the G2 Charles H. Strub Stakes at Santa Anita. He finished the race fourth, ten, and three quarters behind.

A month later Tapizar tried another track when he went to Oaklawn Park for the Razorback Handicap.

Tapizar lost this race by one and a half lengths at the finish to take second.

He returned in the West Virginia Governor's Stakes where he won by four and a half lengths.

His final race before his second chance at the Breeders' Cup Dirt Mile was another disappointment when he came in 6th place, 20 3/4 lengths behind.

Then he came to the last race of his career, the 2012 Breeders' Cup Dirt Mile.

He finished in fifth place the year before but this time he won by two and a quarter lengths.

The following year, Tapizar was retired to stud with a race record of 14 starts, 6 wins, 1 second-place finish, and 1 third-place finish, and grossing $972,632.

On March 26, 2015, Tapizar with Dam, Drumette, sired the 2018 Kentucky Oaks winner Monomoy Girl.

With a champion racehorse like Monomoy Girl as one of his foals, he was a sought-after stud.

Tapizar had been sold to stand as a stud to Yushun Stallion Station in Niikappu District, Hokkaido Japan, and was scheduled to be shipped to their stables in mid-January of 2021.

On December 15, 2020, Tapizar suffered a stall accident in his stall at the Gainesway quarantine barn in Lexington Kentucky just one month before his scheduled trip to Japan, and was euthanized.

At the time of his death, Tapizar has sired 12 stakes winners from 482 named foals of racing age. His progeny have collectively earned more than $22.5 million.

Drumette, Dam of Monomoy Girl, was named the 2020 Kentucky Broodmare of the Year.

Monomoy Girl's Dam, Drumette was born in 2008. Her Sire is Henny Hughes and her Dam is Endless Parade.

Drumette's pedigree includes such notable horses as Secretariat, Seattle Slew, and Bold Ruler.

Henny Hughes is the son of Hennessy out of the mare Meadow Flyer. Henny Hughes' sire, Hennessy, is a son of Storm Cat who was the leading sire in North America in 1999 and 2000.

Storm Cat was also the leading broodmare sire in North America in 2012, 2013, and 2014.

At the time of Storm Cat's death in April 2013, he had sired 8 champions, 35 grade/group one winners, 108 winners of a group or graded stakes races, and 180 stakes winners worldwide, which have earned over $128 million.

Her Grand Sire Williamstown is a son of Seattle Slew.

Seattle Slew is in both Monomoy Girl's Sire and Dam's bloodlines.

Williamstown is also the sire of Grade III winner Vinemeister and 15 other stakes winners.

Drumette was named 2020 Broodmare of the Year at the Kentucky Thoroughbred Owners and Breeders and Kentucky Thoroughbred Association's Kentucky-bred Champions awards presentation.

Drumette's produce record was also bolstered in 2020 by Mr. Monomoy, a colt by Palace Malice who won the G2 Risen Star Stakes and finished third in the G3 Lecomte Stakes held at the Fair Grounds Race Course in New Orleans, Louisiana.

Other runners contributing to Drumette's record in 2020 included Cowboy Diplomacy (by Tapizar) and Superman Shaq (by Shackleford).

Drumette has a 2-year-old filly from the first crop of Mastert, a yearling colt by Tapit, and she was booked back to Tapit for 2021.

Here is a breakdown of Monomoy Girl's pedigree back to Seattle Slew on her Sire's side.

The names at the top of the chart represent Monomoy Girl's

Sire's pedigree / Dam's pedigree

1ST & 2ND GENERATION
TAPIT / HENNY HUGHES

MONOMOY GIRL
ch 2015
THOROUGHBRED

TAPIZAR
b 17.0H 2008
THOROUGHBRED

TAPIT
gr 16.0 2001
THOROUGHBRED
(USA)

WINNING CALL
b 1998
THOROUGHBRED

DRUMETTE
b 2008
THOROUGHBRED

HENNY HUGHES
ch 2003
THOROUGHBRED

ENDLESS PARADE
dkb/br 1997
THOROUGHBRED

3RD GENERATION
PULPIT / HENNESSY

TAPIT gr 16.0 2001 THOROUGHBRED (USA)	PULPIT b 16.0 1994 THOROUGHBRED (USA)
	TAP YOUR HEELS gr 1996 THOROUGHBRED (USA)
WINNING CALL b 1998 THOROUGHBRED	DEPUTY MINISTER b 1979 THOROUGHBRED (CAN)
	CALL NOW br 1992 THOROUGHBRED
HENNY HUGHES ch 2003 THOROUGHBRED	HENNESSY ch 1993 THOROUGHBRED (USA)
	MEADOW FLYER 1989 THOROUGHBRED
ENDLESS PARADE dkb/br 1997 THOROUGHBRED	WILLIAMSTOWN dkb/br 1990 THOROUGHBRED
	MNEMOSYNE b 1989 THOROUGHBRED

4TH GENERATION
AP INDY / STORM CAT

PULPIT b 16.0 1994 THOROUGHBRED (USA)	AP INDY dkb/br 16.0 1989
	PREACH b 1989
TAP YOUR HEELS gr 1996 THOROUGHBRED (USA)	UNBRIDLED b 16.3 1987
	RUBY SLIPPERS gr 1982
DEPUTY MINISTER b 1979 THOROUGHBRED (CAN)	VICE REGENT ch 1967
	MINT COPY b 1970
CALL NOW br 1992 THOROUGHBRED	WILD AGAIN blk 15.3 1980
	CAROLS CHRISTMAS dkb/br 1977
HENNESSY ch 1993 THOROUGHBRED (USA)	STORM CAT br 16.0 1983
	ISLAND KITTY ch 1976
MEADOW FLYER 1989 THOROUGHBRED	MEADOWLAKE ch 17.0 1983
	SHORTLEY 1980
WILLIAMSTOWN dkb/br 1990 THOROUGHBRED	SEATTLE SLEW br 16.0 1974
	WINTER SPARKLE b 1983
MNEMOSYNE b 1989 THOROUGHBRED	SARATOGA SIX b 1982
	MY LADY LOVE b 1981

5TH GENERATION
SEATTLE SLEW / STORM BIRD

AP INDY dkb/br 16.0 1989	SEATTLE SLEW	br 16.0 1974
	WEEKEND SURPRISE	b 1980
PREACH b 1989	MR. PROSPECTOR	b 16.0 1970
	NARRATE	br 1980
UNBRIDLED b 16.3 1987	FAPPIANO	b 16.2 1977
	GANA FACIL	ch 1981
RUBY SLIPPERS gr 1982	NIJINSKY	b 16.3 1967
	MOON GLITTER	gr 1980
VICE REGENT ch 1967	NORTHERN DANCER	b 15.1 1961
	VICTORIA REGINA	ch 1958
MINT COPY b 1970	BUNTYS FLIGHT	b 1953
	SHAKNEY	dkb/br 1964
WILD AGAIN blk 15.3 1980	ICECAPADE	gr 1969
	BUSHEL-N-PECK	br 1958
CAROLS CHRISTMAS dkb/br 1977	WHITESBURG	ch 1969
	LIGHT VERSE	b 1970
STORM CAT br 16.0 1983	STORM BIRD	b 1978
	TERLINGUA	ch 1978
ISLAND KITTY ch 1976	HAWAII	b 16.1 1964
	T C KITTEN	ch 1969
MEADOWLAKE ch 17.0 1983	HOLD YOUR PEACE	b 1969
	SUSPICIOUS NATIVE	ch 1972
SHORTLEY 1980	HAGLEY	b 1967
	SHORT WINDED	b 1965
SEATTLE SLEW br 16.0 1974	BOLD REASONING	dkb/br 1968
	MY CHARMER	b 16.1 1969
WINTER SPARKLE b 1983	NORTHJET	ch 1977
	TURN TO TALENT	b 1963
SARATOGA SIX b 1982	ALYDAR	dk ch 1975
	PRICELESS FAME	b 1975
MY LADY LOVE b 1981	SMARTEN	br 1976
	LADY DULCINEA	gr 1963

Part Five
Monomoy Girl

Sire: Tapizar

Dam: Drumette

Monomoy Girl was born on March 26, 2015.

She is a chestnut mare with a white star bred in Kentucky by FPF LLC & Highfield Ranch.

Her pedigree through her sire is a list of champion horses.

When she was born it was expected that she would be a great racehorse. But nobody could imagine how great she would eventually become.

Monomoy Girl showed very promising form as a juvenile in 2017 when she won her first three races before being narrowly beaten in the Golden Rod Stakes.

Her maiden race was race #6 at the Indiana Grand Race Course, Maiden Special Weight on September, 5th, 2017 in Shelbyville, Indiana as the 3-2 favorite.

This race was a 1-mile turf race. She broke slowly out of the gate and was carried six wide around the final turn and she won by 3-¾ lengths with a time of 1:42.31. Her jockey for this race was Marcelino Pedroza.

They won the $18,600 purse.

The second place was taken by Lemon Princess, followed by She Might Tell.

Monomoy Girl's second race was the Allowance Optional Claiming at Churchill Downs in Louisville Kentucky, on Thursday, September 28th, 2017.

This was the 7th race of the night.

This race was for two year-old fillies who have never won two races or claiming $75,000.

When the one-mile race started at 7:58 that evening, Monomoy Girl's trainer, Brad Cox knew that this was going to be the racetrack to win at.

Monomoy Girl and her new jockey, Florent Geroux did not disappoint Cox.

Monomoy Girl won by 1-1/4 lengths in a final time of 1:37.87. This time was five seconds faster than her first race at the Indiana Grand Race Course.

Moonlight Rain came in second followed by Malibu Saint.

The winning purse for this race was $31,800.

Monomoy Girl had a month off to train before her next race which would also be run at Churchill Downs on October 29th.

The Rags to Riches Stakes (Black Type) race was the 8th race of the day at Churchill Downs and her first race on dirt.

It was a cloudy day in Louisville and many were praying that the rain would not come before the race was finished.

At 4:29 the horses were off and Monomoy Girl took the lead soon after the start and drew away in the straight to win in a time of 1:36.29, Monomoy Girl and Florent Geroux crossed the finish line in first place winning by 6-1/2 lengths.

She was followed by Queen Mum and Foxtrot sally.

The winning purse for Monomoy Girl for this win was $48,950.

Monomoy Girl was now three wins for three races and has earned a total of $99,350.

Florent Geroux and Monomoy Girl's final race of her maiden season was on November 25th, in The Golden Rod Stakes where she was stepped up to Grade II class at Churchill Downs.

With her two previous wins at Churchill Downs, many people believed that Monomoy Girl would be a sure bet for this 1-1/16 mile dirt track.

The Golden Rod Stakes Grade 2 race was the 9th race of the day.

Monomoy Girl started the odds-on favorite in a field of twelve horses.

When the gates opened at 4:50 p.m. she quickly went to the front, with Road to Victory in a close second.

As they turned into the stretch, Monomoy Girl opened up a lead of 1-1/2 lengths and looked as though she would be the winner.

But unfortunately, she started to weave from side to side late in the race, and Road to Victory caught her in the final strides.

When the race finished in a time of 1:43.6, Monomoy Girls had her first loss in her racing career.

Road to Victory won the race and Monomoy Girl lost by a head followed by Cash Out.

Even with the second-place finish, she walked away with a $37,200 purse.

By the end of her first racing season, Monomoy Girl had won $136,550 in race winnings with a record of 3 wins and 1 loss.

2018 Season

Now that Monomoy Girl was going to be three years old she could race in the Kentucky Oaks race at Churchill Downs on May 4th.

She just had to get through the first two races (legs) in her, "Road to the Kentucky Oaks".

The Road to the Kentucky Oaks is a points system where Thoroughbred fillies qualify for the Kentucky Oaks, held on the first Friday of May, the day before the Kentucky Derby.

The races are held from September 2017, when the fillies were age two, through April 2018, when they turned three years old.

The top four finishers in the specified races earned points, with the highest point values awarded in the major races held in late March or early April.

Monomoy Girl's second race season started with her first, on February 17th at the Rachel Alexandra Stakes (Grade. 2) race for three-year-old fillies, at Fair Grounds Race Course located in New Orleans.

The horses were off at 4:13 that afternoon. Monomoy Girl broke out then hit the gate and was the last horse to commence.

When the horses made it to the first turn, Monomoy Girl was at the back of the pack.

When they made their way to the half-mile pole Monomoy Girl moved out of the last place as the horses rallied four wide on the far turn.

She kept on pretty well in the final furlong.

With a final race time of 1:43.26, Monomoy and Florent crossed the finish line in first place followed by 2 1/2 lengths was Classy Act in second and Wonder Gadot pulling up third.

Her first race was a success and she won the $120,000 purse.

Brad Cox and Florent Geroux felt that the rest of the 2018 race season looked promising.

Monomoy Girl left Louisiana and headed back to Lexington Kentucky for the April 7th Central Bank Ashland Stakes (Grade. 1) at Keeneland.

The race was the 9th race on the schedule that day. And at 5:48 the gates opened and unlike her last start, Monomoy Girl came out strong.

They were running four-wide through the second turn and into the stretch.

When the race finished in a time of 1:43.74, Monomoy Girl won by 5 1/2 lengths to win the $300,000 purse.

Second place was won by Eskimo Kisses and the third-place finisher was Patrona Margarita.

With her first two races being a success and the 5 1/2 length win in Keeneland, Brad Cox and Florent Geroux knew that she was ready for the biggest race of her career, The Longines Kentucky Oaks at Churchill Downs on May 4th.

The Longines Kentucky Oaks is a Grade I stakes race for three-year-old Thoroughbred fillies that is run annually at Churchill Downs in Louisville, Kentucky.

It is considered by some to be among the most popular horse races in American horse racing. The attendance of the Longines Kentucky Oaks typically only trails the Kentucky Derby and the Preakness Stakes.

The race is 1-1/8 miles in length and the horses carry 121 pounds.

The Longines Kentucky Oaks is held on the Friday before the Kentucky Derby each year. The winner gets a large garland blanket of lilies, called the "Lillies for the Fillies."

The winner also receives the silver Kentucky Oaks Trophy.

And just as the Kentucky Derby race for three-year-old male Thoroughbreds is part of the "Tipple Crown". For a horse to be the Triple Crown winner they must win The Kentucky Derby, Preakness Stakes, and Belmont Stakes.

The fillies have a similar race called the "Triple Tiara" formerly known as "The Filly Triple Crown".

The only official Triple Tiara is a series of three races in New York.

They are: The Acorn Stakes run at Belmont Park, The Coaching Club American Oaks, run at Saratoga Race Course, and The Alabama Stakes, also run at Saratoga.

There are talks to create a "National Triple Tiara" and is being considered to be three races that are on the undercard of the three Triple Crown races.

Monomoy Girl was the favorite at 2-1 odds and started on the outside in the 14th post, with Midnight Bisou at 5-2 starting in 10th position in a field of 14.

Brad Cox had a second horse running in that race also. Sassy Sienna was starting in the 1st position.

When the gates opened for the Longines Kentucky Oaks, Take Charge Paula held the lead for the first half-mile.

Monomoy Girl took the lead around the halfway point of the race and Wonder Gadot, at 16-1 made a hard charge down the stretch.

Florent Geroux and Monomoy Girl pulled away and won the Longines Kentucky Oaks by half a length in a time of 1:49.13

This was the first Kentucky Oaks win for trainer Brad Cox and the payout for this win was $564,200.

Wonder Gadot came in second and Midnight Bisou, the 2-1 favorite, overcame a slow start to make a late run, but only finished third.

Monomoy Girl was now headed to The Acorn Stakes at Belmont Park.

Monomoy Girl arrived at the Belmont racetrack On June 9th, 26 days after her win at the Longines Kentucky Oaks.

The Acorn Stakes is raced on dirt over a distance of one mile. And this is in Monomoy Girl's favor as she is undefeated in 1-mile races.

Owned by Michael Dubb, Monomoy Stables, The Elkstone Group, and Bethlehem Stables, Monomoy Girl is three-for-three in her 2018 race season.

When the race started Monomoy Girl sat behind the pace of Moonshine Memories and Talk Veuve to Me through three quarters before drawing off and winning by two lengths in 1:34.10.

Talk Veuve to Me ran well to maintain second followed by Gio Game who ran third.

Moonshine Memories eventually faded back to finish fourth.

The winning purse for this race was $375,000.

The win at The Acorn Stakes put Monomoy Girl's win streak to four races during her three-year-old campaign.

She was only halfway through her three-year-old campaign.

Monomoy Girl's record now is 8-7-1-0, and $1,495,750 career mark and is the first registered stakes winner out of the Henny Hughes mare, Drumette, who is a half-sister to Grade 3 victor Drum Major.

Monomoy Girl's next race was scheduled for July 22nd, at the Coaching Club American Oaks Grade 1 race in Saratoga New York.

She was set to face off against Midnight Bisou, Chocolate Martini, Eskimo Kisses, and Gio Game.

When the race started Monomoy Girl lead the race on the first turn. And she stayed in the lead pack for the duration of the race.

The final time was 1:50.46 with Monomoy Girl winning by three lengths, followed by Midnight Bisou and Chocolate Martini.

Monomoy Girl had a two-month break between the Coaching Club American Oaks Grade 1 and the Cotillion Stakes Grade 1 at Parx Racecourse in Bensalem, Pennsylvania on September 22nd.

It was a cloudy Saturday at Parx Racing when the race started at 4:56.

Monomoy Girl had the number two pole position. Monomoy Girl took the lead when the gates opened.

When the race was finished 1:45.95 later it looked as though Monomoy Girl had won yet another race.

However, following a claim of foul by Mike Smith, the rider of Midnight Bisou for interference in the stretch, she was disqualified.

Monomoy Girl was placed second and Wonder Gadot finished in third.

The Cotillion Stakes Grade 1 loss was the first loss in Monomoy Girl's three-year-old race season.

And with the Breeders' Cup Longines Distaff (Grade 1) race next, everyone hoped it would be her last.

The final race for Monomoy Girl in her 2018 race season was Breeders' Cup Longines Distaff (Grade 1) at Churchill Downs Racetrack in Louisville, Kentucky.

Monomoy Girl faced older fillies and mares for the first time in the Breeders' Cup Distaff on November 3rd, at Churchill Downs.

Monomoy Girl started at the 11th pole position.

She quickly broke from the outside post and stalked the early pace set by Wonder Gadot then took command rounding the turn.

She held off a late run from Wow Cat in the final stretch and won by a length in a final time of 1:49.79.

The winning purse for the race was $1,100,000, bringing her winnings for her 2018 race seasons to $218,200,000.

Monomoy Girl was named the champion three-year-old filly of 2018, earning all but two votes in her Eclipse Award category of Three-Year-Old Filly.

The Eclipse Award was established in 1971 and named after the great 18th-Century racehorse and sire Eclipse, who was undefeated in 18 starts.

The Eclipse Awards are presented annually to recognize Thoroughbred horses and individuals whose achievements have earned them the title of Champion in their respective categories, and to members of the media for outstanding coverage of Thoroughbred racing.

In the Top 100 Rankings for 2018; Monomoy Girl was ranked 61st by wins and ranked 4th by earnings.

2019 Season

Monomoy Girl did not race at age four after suffering a mild case of colic that was expected to sideline her for about three weeks.

At first, it was believed that the colic would only prevent her from making her 4-year-old debut on May 3rd, 2019 in the $500,000 La Troienne Stakes (Grade 1) at Churchill Downs.

It was first noticed that something wasn't right with Monomoy Girl when she exited a van ride from Fair Grounds Race Course & Slots to Churchill in the last week of March with an upset stomach.

She then received several days of treatment at Rood and Riddle Equine Hospital in Lexington for dehydration.

After Monomoy Girl's treatment for dehydration, she was sent to WinStar Farm near Versailles, Ky., to recover.

Everyone hoped to have her back in good health by May 1.

Her trainer Brad Cox said that he will not decide on her next start until "she puts in a good (five-furlong workout)."

As it turned out Monomoy Girl was not able to race at all in her four-year-old season.

All of her supporters were waiting patiently for 2020.

2020 Season

In 2020, she did not disappoint her supporters.

The first race of her five-year-old season was on 5/16/2020 at Churchill Downs as the 1-2 favorite when she ran the Allowance Optional Claiming.

The race was started at 2:34 and Monomoy Girl was in the 2 pole position.

She ran two-wide around the first turn and then went three-wide around the final turn.

The race was well worth the wait as Monomoy Girl and Florent crossed the finish line in the first place by 2 $\frac{3}{4}$ lengths in a time of 1:36.51.

The second place was taken by Red Dane followed by Miss Bigly.

It was a great start to her 2020 race season; 1 win and a purse of $48,868.

She won the 1-mile race in 2 ¾ lengths.

Monomoy Girl has been a great horse running the 1-mile tracks. And Brad Cox knew that he had a great chance of winning their next race, the Ruffian Stakes (Grade 2), at Belmont in just 2 months on July 11th.

If Monomoy Girl wins this race it would be the first time that a horse trained by Cox would win the Ruffian Stakes (Grade 2).

When Monomoy Girl arrived at Belmont Park for the Ruffian Stakes (Grade 2), she was ready to race.

The Ruffian Stakes (Grade 2) was started at 2:57.

In the first half of the race, Monomoy Girl was just holding her own and running about five wide down the backstretch and four wide around the turn. Then around the quarter pole, she was four to five wide into the upper stretch.

She eventually pulled out to take the lead clear to the finish.

Winning the Ruffian Stakes (Grade 2) by two lengths, in a time of 1:34.13 and taking home the $82,500 purse.

She was now heading back to Churchill Downs for the September 4th, La Troienne Stakes, and a second Breeders' Cup Distaff on November 7th.

Many people believed that these next two races would be wins as she has only lost 1 time in 7 races at Churchill Downs.

At the La Troienne Stakes, Monomoy Girl got off to a slow start and as they went into the first turn she bumped with Risky Mandate.

In the final turn, she started her move and moved to the lead in mid-stretch.

At odds of 2-5, Monomoy Girl did what everyone expected. She won the 1 1/16 mile race by 1 ¾ length in a time of 1:42.14.

She was followed by Lady Kate and Horologist.

The winning purse for this race was $300,700.

After this win, she would have a two-month break before running in the 2020 Breeders' Cup Distaff (Grade 1) at Keeneland, on November 7th.

This would be the second time that Monomoy Girl would race in the Breeders' Cup Distaff (Grade 1).

This time she had an opponent that stood out as real competition, a three-year-old filly Swiss Skydiver.

This would be Swiss Skydiver's 10th race of the season with a record of 5 wins and 4 losses.

Just one month earlier on October 16, she won the Preakness Grade 1 race beating out Authentic by a short neck, who won the 2020 Kentucky Derby.

Even though Monomoy Girl was the even-money favorite, this would be a race between two amazing horses.

When the horses loaded up in their gates that afternoon only three other horses have won the Breeders' Cup Distaff (Grade 1) twice in their racing career.

They were:

Bayakoa (ARG) 1989-1990

Royal Delta 2011-2012

Beholder 2013-2016

Monomoy Girl already won this race in her 2018 season. And she was just 1 1/8 mile from being the fourth horse to do so.

The gates opened at 3:55 and the 2020 Breeders' Cup Distaff (Grade 1) was running.

Monomoy Girl broke well from the outside post and settled in the fourth position behind Lady Kate and Harvest Moon.

However, the one horse that people felt could compete with Monomoy Girl, Swiss Skydiver, stumbled out of the starting gate and fell into eighth place.

On the final turn, Swiss Skydiver made up ground on the rail while Monomoy Girl circled the field on the outside.

The two battled briefly before Swiss Skydiver tired and fell back into the seventh position.

Monomoy Girl held off a late run from Valiance and Dunbar Road.

And after 1:47.84 Monomoy Girl and Florent Geroux crossed the finish line in the first place. Followed by 1 ¾ length by Valiance and in third was Dunbar Road.

Swiss Skydiver finished in seventh place.

The winning purse was $1,040,000.

This brought here 2020 winnings total to $1,472,068.

At the end of her 2020 season, Monomoy Girl was six in earnings among the all-time North American-based dirt females with $4,426,818 and ranked 7th overall in earnings in the top 100.

She has won 13 of her 15 starts to date for owners Michael Dubb, Monomoy Stables, The Elkstone Group (Stuart Grant), and Bethlehem Stables and trainer Brad Cox.

She was within a neck of victory in her other two starts.

This was Monomoy Girl's final race for her 2020 racing season.

Following the Breeders' Cup Distaff (Grade 1) Monomoy Girl was loaded up and traveled just 1 hour east of Churchill Downs to the Fasig-Tipton auction in Lexington, Kentucky, where she was offered as a broodmare or racing prospect at the "Night of the Stars" sale.

She made her way to the auction ring with hip tag # 192.

The seven-time Grade 1 winner was purchased by Spendthrift Farm for $9,500,000 from the consignment of ELiTE, agent.

Her 9.5 million dollar price, tied with Songbird as the third-highest price ever offered for a filly or mare.

Monomoy Girl earned her second Eclipse Award in her 2020 racing season, taking the Older Dirt Female title after being voted the 2018 Champion Three-Year-Old Filly.

Monomoy Girl's trainer, Brad Cox, earned his first Eclipse Award for Outstanding Trainer after being a finalist in 2019.

Cox finished second in overall trainer earnings with more than $18.9 million in 2020.

He won 30 graded stakes and tied the record for most wins at one Breeders' Cup by a trainer with four at last year's World Championships.

In addition to training Monomoy Girl in the Distaff, Brad Cox trained Shedaresthedevil to victory in the Longines Kentucky Oaks (Grade 1) at Churchill Downs. (The same race that Monomoy Girl won in 2018.)

Her new owners, My Racehorse Stable, Spendthrift Farm LLC, and Madaket Stables LLC decided to keep her and jockey Florent Geroux in training together.

MyRacehorse Stable in turn offered micro-shares of her to the general public.

Sol Kumin also bought back a minority share.

In May 2018, he became the first owner since 1952 to have a Kentucky Oaks (Monomoy Girl) and Kentucky Derby winner (Justify) in the same weekend.

2021 Season

Monomoy Girl's six-year-old season will most likely be her last.

Her first six-year-old debut race was postponed when Oaklawn Park had to cancel racing in mid-February due to severe winter weather.

The 1 $\frac{1}{16}$ mile, Bayakoa Stakes, is usually run in the third week of February but was moved to February 28th.

Monomoy Girl held a 1-5 odds in a field of six.

When the gates opened she stalked the early pace while racing four-wide, and then took the lead at the head of the stretch.

She won by two lengths with a time of 1:45.92 and took home the $150,000 purse.

On April 15th, one of Monomoy Girl's owners, MyRacehorse of Claremont, CA. offered 10,200 shares of Monomoy Girl to the public for $46.00 per share that held 0.0050% Equity Per Share.

MyRacehorse is a 51% owner in Monomoy Girl.

She now had seven weeks off before her next big race of 2020, the Apple Blossom Handicap on April 17th, where she would once again face Swiss Skydiver.

The 1 $\frac{1}{16}$ mile Apple Blossom Handicap was billed as a match race against Swiss Skydiver.

The Apple Blossom Handicap is for fillies that are four- years- old and older.

The field of only six horses left out of the gate at 6:12.

Monomoy Girl who started in the 6th pole position was away in good order, behind leader Letruska and Swiss Skydiver.

Monomoy Girl made her way to the front with a furlong out and continued to hold until the final stretch.

It was a battle of mere inches down to the wire where Monomoy Girl lost by a nose to the 2019 Champion Mexican Three-Year-Old filly Letruska, in a final time of 1:43.14.

Swiss Skydiver finished in third; once again being beat to the finish line by Monomoy Girl.

Some people believe that Letruska had the advantage by a six-pound difference between her and Monomoy Girl (124-118).

Monomoy Girl's future has been in limbo since her second-place loss at the Apple Blossom Handicap.

On May 7th, Monomoy Girl's owners decided to give a brief break from training, with the expectation of her returning for a second-half of the year campaign on the racetrack.

Monomoy Girl didn't bounce out of her second-place finish in the Grade 1 Apple Blossom Handicap as quickly as they would have hoped.

They said that while there are no serious physical issues with Monomoy Girl, she recently has been experiencing some minor muscle strains and hamstring soreness.

After a thorough veterinary workup, her owners were advised that giving Monomoy Girl a short break from training would be very beneficial.

Her owners have said that Monomoy Girl will remain at WinStar Farm in Kentucky, where she will be turned out for 30 days while being hand-walked while she recovers from muscle soreness.

Her veterinarian, Dr. Wes Sutter of Kentucky Equine Hospital, has also cleared Monomoy Girl to begin a swimming regime in two weeks.

Monomoy Girl is being treated by the Hyperbaric Chamber as a part of the treatment plan.

The Hyperbaric Chamber is used as oxygen therapy to promote and aid in her healing process.

She will use the Hyperbaric Chamber until she has been treated for five consecutive days, followed by five more treatments every other day.

Once Monomoy Girl completes her Hyperbaric Chamber therapy, she will likely begin using the underwater treadmill at WinStar to maintain her fitness without over-exerting her muscles.

Spendthrift general manager Ned Toffey said, "We fully expect Monomoy Girl to return for a second-half of the year campaign and anticipate more terrific performances to come from our wonderful mare."

It was also stated that they are happy that she will be spending her turnout time at WinStar, which has an amazing facility for horses who are getting a break from training. And they look forward to getting Monomoy Girl back to Brad's barn after this brief respite, which they believe will do her a world of good.

It was also said that Monomoy Girl is turned out daily in a round pen to enjoy the great Kentucky bluegrass and natural vitamin D from the sun at 9 a.m. until it's time for her afternoon feed at 3 p.m.

Many of her supporters and are hoping for a positive and full recovery and her return to the race track to finish out her 2020 season.

But the memory of her 2019 season is still fresh in their minds.